Why Why Why do magnets push and pull?

MC
PUBLISHERS

First published as hardback in 2006 by
Miles Kelly Publishing Ltd, Bardfield Centre,
Great Bardfield, Essex, CM7 4SLCopyright
© Miles Kelly Publishing Ltd 2006

This 2009 edition published and distributed
by:

Mason Crest Publishers Inc.
370 Reed Road, Broomall, Pennsylvania
19008
(866) MCP-BOOK (toll free)
www.masoncrest.com

Why Why Why—
Do Magnets Push and Pull?
ISBN 978-1-4222-1583-8
Library of Congress Cataloging-in-
Publication data is available

Why Why Why—?
Complete 23 Title Series
ISBN 978-1-4222-1568-5

Printed in the United States of America

Contents

Is science in the playground?

Yes, it is! Lots of science happens in a playground. The playground rides could not work without science. A see-saw is a simple machine called a lever. It has a long arm and a point in the middle called a pivot. As you ride on the see-saw, the lever tips up and down on the pivot.

See-saw

Lever

Pivot

Sloping machine!

A ramp is the simplest machine of all. It is easier to walk up a ramp to the top of a hill than it is to climb a steep hillside.

What is a wheel?

A wheel is a very simple machine that can spin around. Wheels let other machines, such as skateboards, bicycles, cars and trains, roll along smoothly. They also make it easy to move heavy weights in carts and wheelbarrows.

What makes things stop and start?

Pushes and pulls make things stop and start. Scientists use the word 'force' for pushes and pulls. Forces are all around us. The force of gravity pulls things downwards. It makes a rollercoaster car hurtle downhill. It also slows the car on the uphill parts of the track.

Feel

Press the palm of your hand onto a table. A force called friction stops you sliding your hand along.

Rollercoaster

Why do fireworks flash and bang?

Fireworks flash and bang because they are full of chemicals that burn. The chemicals have lots of energy stored in them. When they burn, the energy changes to light, heat and sound. We use chemicals that burn in other places too, such as cookers, heaters and car engines.

Bread

Cheese

Butter

Fireworks

Milk

Fruit and vegetables

Do I need energy?

Yes, you do. Your body needs energy to keep working. It even uses energy when you are fast asleep! You get energy from food. Some food, such as bread, is full of energy. You have to eat other kinds of food as well. They have chemicals in them that keep your body healthy.

Hot! Hot! Hot!

The hottest-ever temperature recorded was in a science laboratory. It was 3.6 billion degrees Fahrenheit (3,600,000,000° F). Now that's hot!

What is a thermometer?

A thermometer tells us how hot something is. This is called temperature. The numbers written on a thermometer are normally degrees Fahrenheit (°F). If you put a thermometer in icy cold water, it shows 32°F. If you put it in boiling water it shows 212°F. A thermometer can also measure your body temperature.

Remember

Look at the picture of food above. Can you remember a food that gives energy?

What is in an electric motor?

Magnets and wires. Electricity from a battery passes through the wires. This turns the wires into a magnet. Two more magnets on each side of the motor push and pull against the wires. This makes a thin metal rod (spindle) spin around.

Battery

Wires

Electricity flows along wires

Magnet on side of motor

Spindle

Where do rainbow colors come from?

The colors of a rainbow are in light that comes from the Sun. This light is called white light. It is made up of lots of colors mixed together. We can see the colors if we send a beam of sunlight through a glass triangle called a prism, or when there's a rainbow in the sky.

Prism

Rainbow colors

Fast as light!

Light is the fastest thing in the Universe. It travels 186,282 miles every second. That means it could travel around the Earth seven times in less than a second!

Make

On a sunny day, stand with your back to the Sun. Spray water into the air and you should see a rainbow!

What is the loudest sound?

The roar of a jet engine is the loudest sound we normally hear. It is thousands of times louder than someone shouting. Sounds this loud can damage our ears if we are too close to them. The quietest sounds we can hear are things like rustling leaves.

Where is science in a city?

Everywhere! In a big city, almost every machine, building and vehicle is based on science. Cars, buses and trains help us move around the city. Scientists and engineers have also worked out how to build tall skyscrapers where people live and work.

City

Look

Look at the city picture. How many different forms of transportation can you see?

Railway signals

Who works railway signals?

Nobody does! The signals work by themselves. Electronic parts on the track work out if a train is passing. Then a computer changes the signals to red, to stop another train moving onto the same piece of track.

How do skyscrapers stay up?

Skyscrapers stay up because they have a strong frame on the inside. The frame is made from steel and concrete. These are very strong materials. Normally you can't see the frame. It is hidden by the skyscraper's walls. The walls hang on the frame.

Plane spotters!

There's science at an airport, too. A radar machine uses radio waves to find aircraft in the sky. This helps people at the airport to guide the aircraft onto the runway.

How do you make magnets?

By using another magnet! Magnets are made from lumps of iron or steel. You can turn a piece of iron into a magnet by stroking it with another magnet. A magnet can also be made by sending electricity through a coil of wire. This is called an electromagnet. Some electromagnets are so strong, they can pick up cars.

Electromagnet picking up scrap cars

Count

Find a magnet at home (you can use a refrigerator magnet). How many paper clips can your magnet pick up?

VR 2314

Does a magnet have a field?

Yes – but it's not a field of grass! The area around a magnet is called a magnetic field. A magnetic field is shown by drawing lines around a magnet. The Earth has a magnetic field, too. It is as though there is a giant magnet inside the Earth.

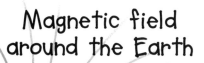
Magnetic field around the Earth

Do magnets push and pull?

Every magnet has two poles. These are where the pull of a magnet is strongest. They are called the north pole and the south pole. A north pole and a south pole always pull toward each other. Two north poles always push each other away. So do two south poles.

Handy rock!

Some rocks act like magnets. Years ago, people used magnetic rocks to find their way. If they let the rock spin round, it always pointed in the same direction.

13

Where does electricity come from?

Battery

Electricity comes to your home along cables from power stations. The cables are held off the ground by towers. Around your home are holes in the wall called sockets. When a machine is plugged into a socket, electricity flows out to work the machine.

Electric!

Our homes are full of machines that work using electricity. If there was no electricity we wouldn't have televisions, lights, washing machines or computers!

Power station

Remember

Electricity is very dangerous. It could kill you. Never play with electric sockets in your home.

What is a circuit?

A circuit is a loop that electricity moves around. This circuit is made up of a battery, a light bulb and a switch. If the switch is turned off, the loop would be broken. Then the electricity would stop moving and the light would go out.

Light bulb

Switch

When is electricity in the sky?

When there's a thunderstorm! During a storm, a kind of electricity called static electricity builds up. This can make a big flash, that lights up the sky. This is lightning. The hot lightning heats up the air around it and this makes a loud clap. This is thunder.

Tower holds cables off the ground

Electricity flows along the cables

What waves are invisible?

Satellite

Radio waves are all around us, but we can't see them. We use radio waves to send sounds and pictures to radios and televisions. Some radio waves come from satellites in space. A radio receives radio waves through a metal rod called an antenna. A dish-shaped antenna picks up radio waves for television programs.

Radio waves

Antenna

Radio

Remember

Which part of your body would stop an X-ray? Skin or bone?

X-ray
machine

Picture
of bone

Dish-shaped
antenna

What is an X-ray?

An X-ray is like a radio wave. X-rays can go through the soft bits of your body. However, hard bones stop them. That's why doctors use X-ray machines to take pictures of the inside of people's bodies.

Space radio!

Radio waves can travel through space. But they can't travel through water. So you can listen to a radio in a space station, but not in a submarine!

What waves can cook food?

Microwaves can. These are a kind of radio wave. They have lots of energy in them. A microwave uses this energy to cook food. Microwaves are fired into the oven. They make the particles in the food vibrate very fast. This makes the food hot.

Are computers clever?

Not really! Computers are amazing machines, but they can only do what they are told. They carry out computer programs written down by people. These are full of instructions that the computer follows. You can also tell a computer what to do by using its keyboard and mouse.

Typing on a keyboard

Mouse

Remember

Can you remember the name for a computer's electronic brain? Read these pages again to help you.

Microchip

Close-up of microchip

Does a computer have a brain?

A computer doesn't have a brain like yours. It has an electronic brain called a central processing unit. This is a microchip the size of your fingernail. This amazing mini machine can do millions of difficult sums in a split second.

Computer

Computer room!

The first computer was made 60 years ago. It was so big that it filled a whole room. A modern calculator can do sums much more quickly!

How does a computer remember?

A computer remembers with its electronic memory. This is made up of lots of tiny microchips. When you turn the computer off, everything in the memory is lost. So you have to save your work on a disc, otherwise you lose it when you switch off.

Is the Internet like a web?

The Internet is made up of millions of computers around the world. They are connected like a giant spider's web! A computer connects to a machine called a modem. This sends signals to a server. The server lets you connect to the Internet. People can send emails and open web pages.

Modem

Email

Find out

Look at the main picture on these pages. See if you can find out what the word 'email' is short for.

What does www stand for?

The letters www are short for World Wide Web. The World Wide Web is like a giant library of information, stored on computers all over the world. There are also thousands of shops on the World Wide Web, where you can buy almost anything.

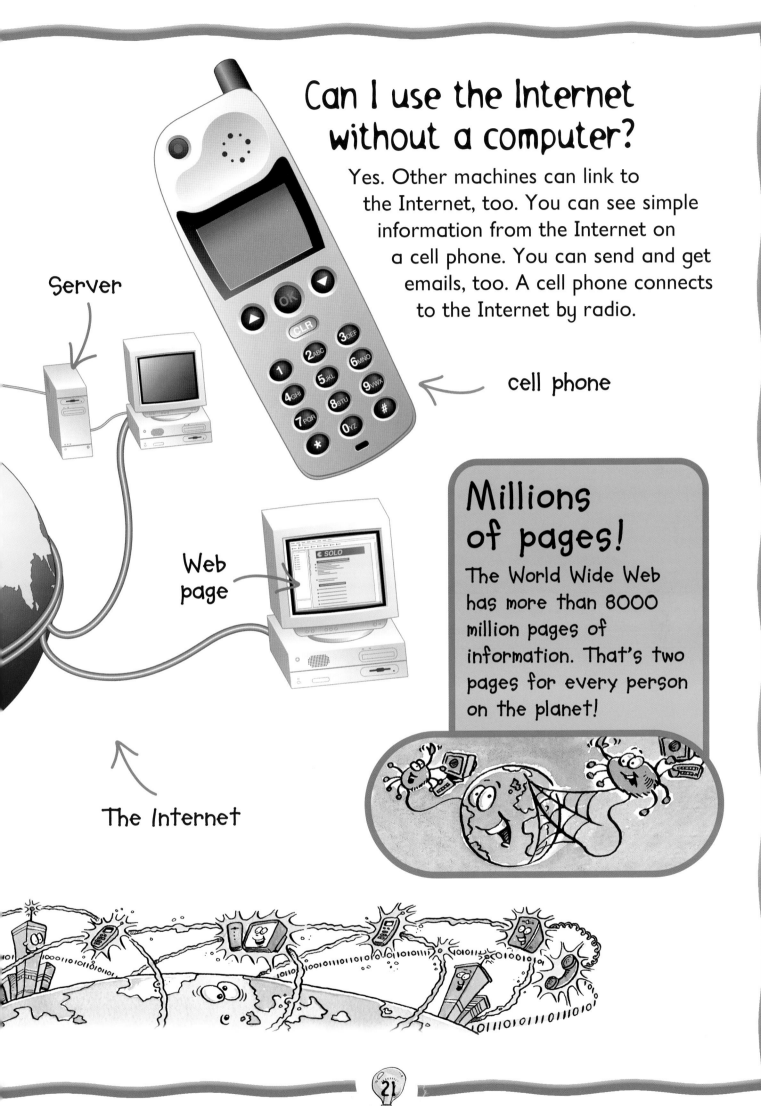

Can I use the Internet without a computer?

Yes. Other machines can link to the Internet, too. You can see simple information from the Internet on a cell phone. You can send and get emails, too. A cell phone connects to the Internet by radio.

Server

cell phone

Web page

The Internet

Millions of pages!

The World Wide Web has more than 8000 million pages of information. That's two pages for every person on the planet!

Can a car be made from cardboard?

Yes, it can – but it would break if you sat inside it! It is always important to use the right material to make something. Cars are made from tough, long-lasting materials. Metal, plastic and rubber are all materials used to make cars.

A racing car is made up of hundreds of parts and different materials

Think

Think of three more materials from which things are made. If you get stuck, ask an adult.

Cotton plants make clothes

What materials grow?

Many of the materials we use every day come from plants. Wood comes from the trunks and branches of trees. Cotton is made from the seeds of cotton plants to make clothes such as t-shirts. Some rubber is made from a liquid (sap) from rubber trees.

Rubber tree makes tires

Tree trunks and branches make wooden bats

Bullet proof!

Some glass is extra-strong. Toughened glass is so hard that even a bullet from a gun bounces off it!

Does glass grow?

Glass doesn't grow! It is made from sand and two other materials called limestone and soda. These materials are mixed together and melted to make a gooey liquid. When the mixture cools down, it forms the hard glass that we use to makes windows, drinking glasses and other objects.

What do scientists do at work?

Some scientists try to find out about the world around us. Others find out about space, planets and stars. Some scientists discover useful materials that we can use. Scientists carry out experiments in laboratories to test their ideas.

Scientist in a laboratory

$=mc^2$

Who is the most famous scientist?

The most famous scientist is called Albert Einstein (1879–1955). He made many discoveries about time, space, the force of gravity and nuclear energy. The ideas that Einstein wrote down were so amazing that they made him famous across the world.

Albert Einstein

Do scientists help doctors?

Yes, they do. Many scientists make medicines that the doctor gives you when you are sick. They also help to make the complicated machines that doctors use in hospitals. Scientists also try to find out what makes us sick, and how we can stay healthy.

Are animals part of science?

Yes, they are! Scientists who study animals and plants work everywhere in the world. They study in hot rainforests, dusty deserts, high mountains, at the freezing poles and in rivers and seas.

Many scientists study animals and plants

Look

Study the picture. Can you see something that might harm the animals and plants?

26

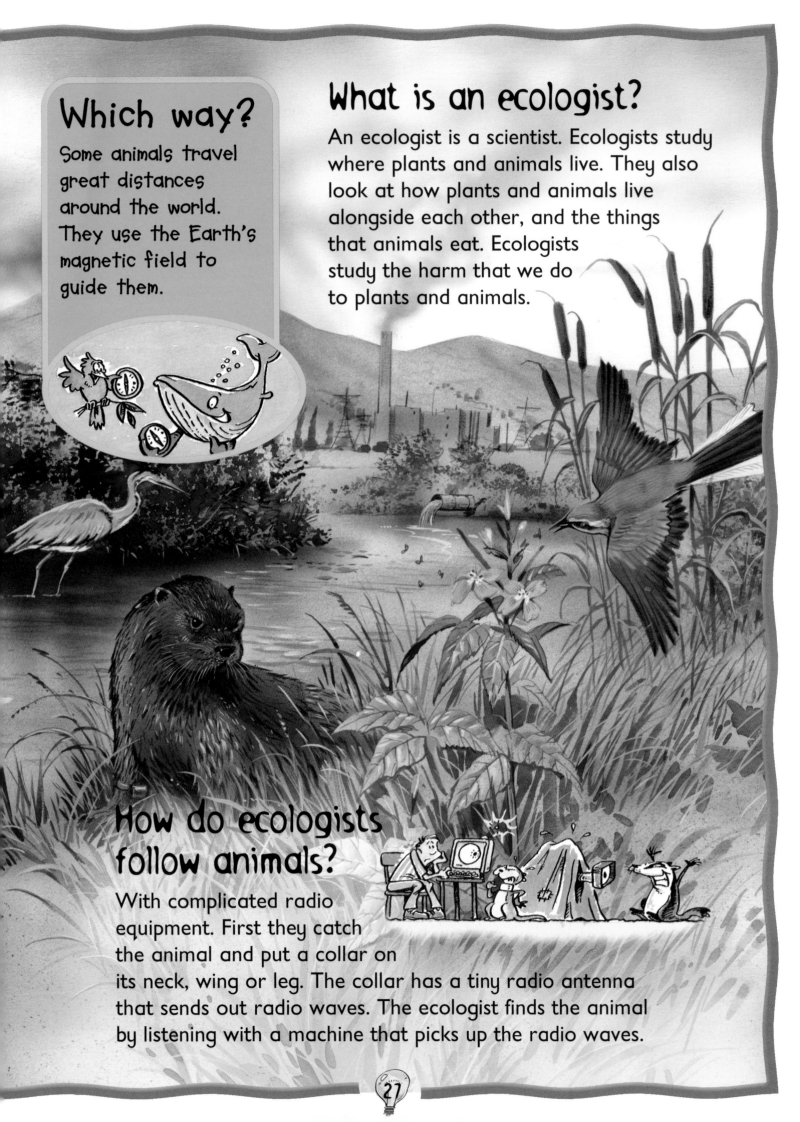

Which way?

Some animals travel great distances around the world. They use the Earth's magnetic field to guide them.

What is an ecologist?

An ecologist is a scientist. Ecologists study where plants and animals live. They also look at how plants and animals live alongside each other, and the things that animals eat. Ecologists study the harm that we do to plants and animals.

How do ecologists follow animals?

With complicated radio equipment. First they catch the animal and put a collar on its neck, wing or leg. The collar has a tiny radio antenna that sends out radio waves. The ecologist finds the animal by listening with a machine that picks up the radio waves.

Are we harming the Earth?

Many of the things we do are harming the world around us. Machines such as cars put dangerous gases into the air. These gases can harm plants and make people ill. They are also making the weather change.

Scientists are always looking for new ways to reduce damage to the Earth.

Pollution

Dirty cars!

Cars and other vehicles can produce so much pollution that in some cities it has become difficult for people to breathe.

What is recycling?

Recycling is using materials again, instead of throwing them away. This helps to make less waste. Ask your parents to take empty glass bottles to a bottle bank. The glass in the bottles is made into new bottles. Paper, metal and plastic are also recycled.

1. Bottle bank

2. Bottles are crushed

3. Glass is melted

4. Liquid glass is put in molds

5. New bottles are ready

Glass recycling

Does electricity harm the Earth?

Yes, it does. Lots of coal, oil and gas are burned to make electricity. These make harmful gases that go into the air. You can help by turning things off to save electricity. Scientists are inventing new ways of making electricity from the wind, the Sun and water.

Save

Ask your family to save electricity. Get them to switch off the lights when nobody is in the room.

Quiz time

Do you remember what you have read about science? These questions will test your memory. The pictures will help you. If you get stuck, read the pages again.

1. Is science in the playground?

page 4

2. Do I need energy?

page 7

3. What is a thermometer?

page 7

page 8

4. What is in an electric motor?

5. How do skyscrapers stay up?

page 11

page 13

6. Does a magnet have a field?

Index